AF483104

Luna falls asleep with a book about Mercury and dreams of flying to the closest planet to the sun.

Hi! I'm Merri

She meets a small and shiny
alien named Merri who shows
her around the planet.

She learns that Mercury has no atmosphere, no moons and a very slow rotation.

She also sees the craters and cliffs that cover the surface of the planet.

She is amazed by how hot and cold the planet can be, depending on the side facing the sun or the dark side.

Luna learns that Mercury is a very unique and extreme planet that has many interesting features.

She also learns that being curious and asking questions can help her discover new things.

Luna falls asleep with a book about Venus and dreams of flying to the second planet from the sun.

Hi! I'm Vena

She meets a beautiful alien
named Vena who shows her
around the planet.

She learns that Venus is the hottest and brightest planet in the solar system, with a thick atmosphere of carbon dioxide and sulfuric acid clouds.

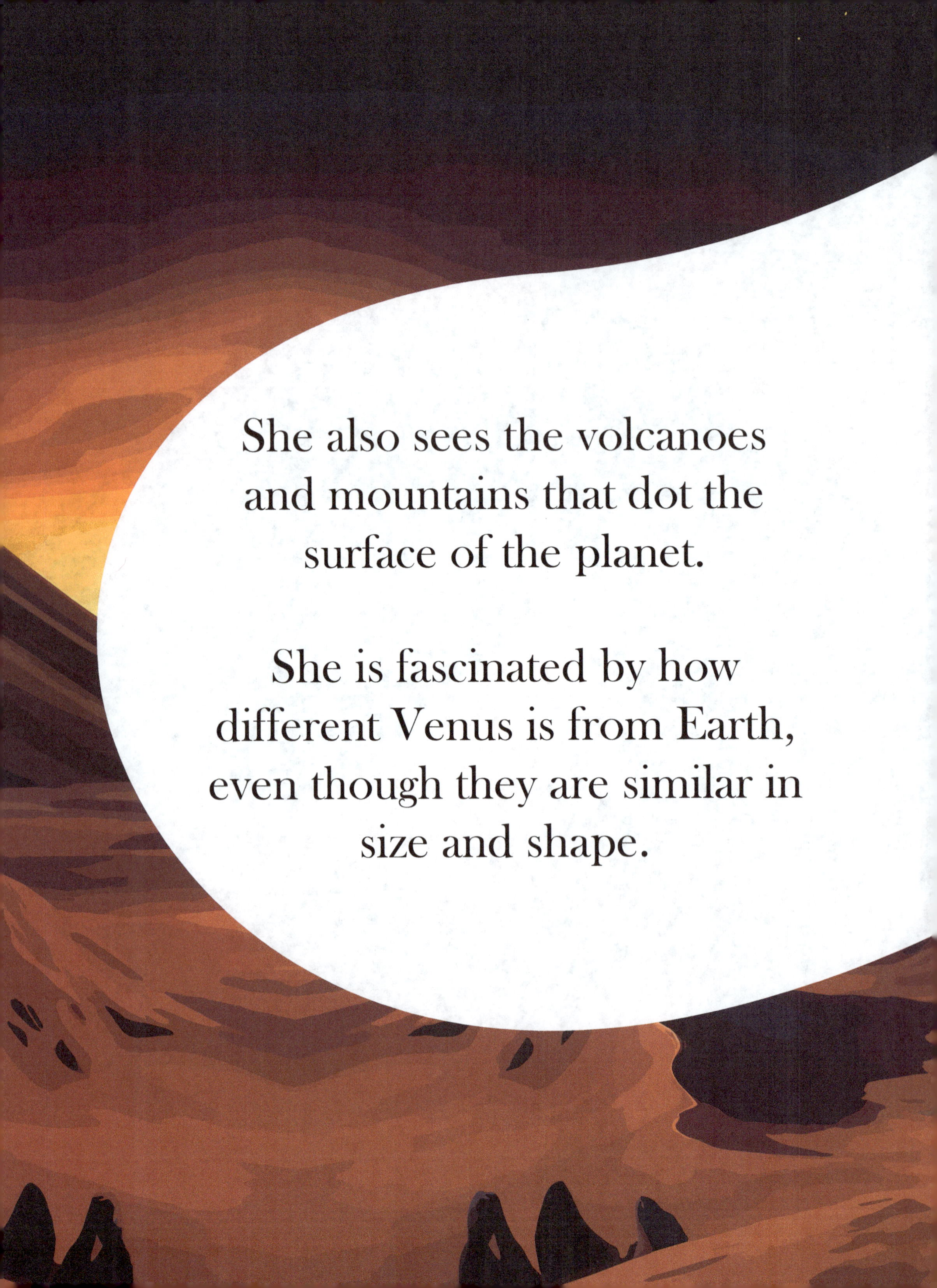

She also sees the volcanoes and mountains that dot the surface of the planet.

She is fascinated by how different Venus is from Earth, even though they are similar in size and shape.

Luna learns that Venus is a very
different and mysterious planet
that has many secrets to reveal.

She also learns that being open
minded and respectful can help
her appreciate the diversity of
the universe.

Luna falls asleep with a book about Saturn and dreams of flying to the sixth planet from the sun.

HI! I'm Sato

She meets a large and friendly
alien named Sato who shows
her around the planet.

She learns that Saturn is the
second largest and most
beautiful planet in the solar
system, with a complex system
of rings and moons.

She also sees the storms and
winds that swirl around the
planet.

She is enchanted by how
majestic and elegant Saturn is,
with its rings and moons.

Luna learns that Saturn is a
very magnificent and graceful
planet that has many wonders
to admire.

She also learns that being
creative and expressive can
help her share her feelings and
thoughts with others.

Luna falls asleep with a book about Mars and dreams of flying to the fourth planet from the sun.

Hi! I'm Marlo

She meets a brave and
adventurous alien named
Marlo who shows her around
the planet.

She learns that Mars is the most Earth like planet in the solar system, with a thin atmosphere, polar caps and seasons.

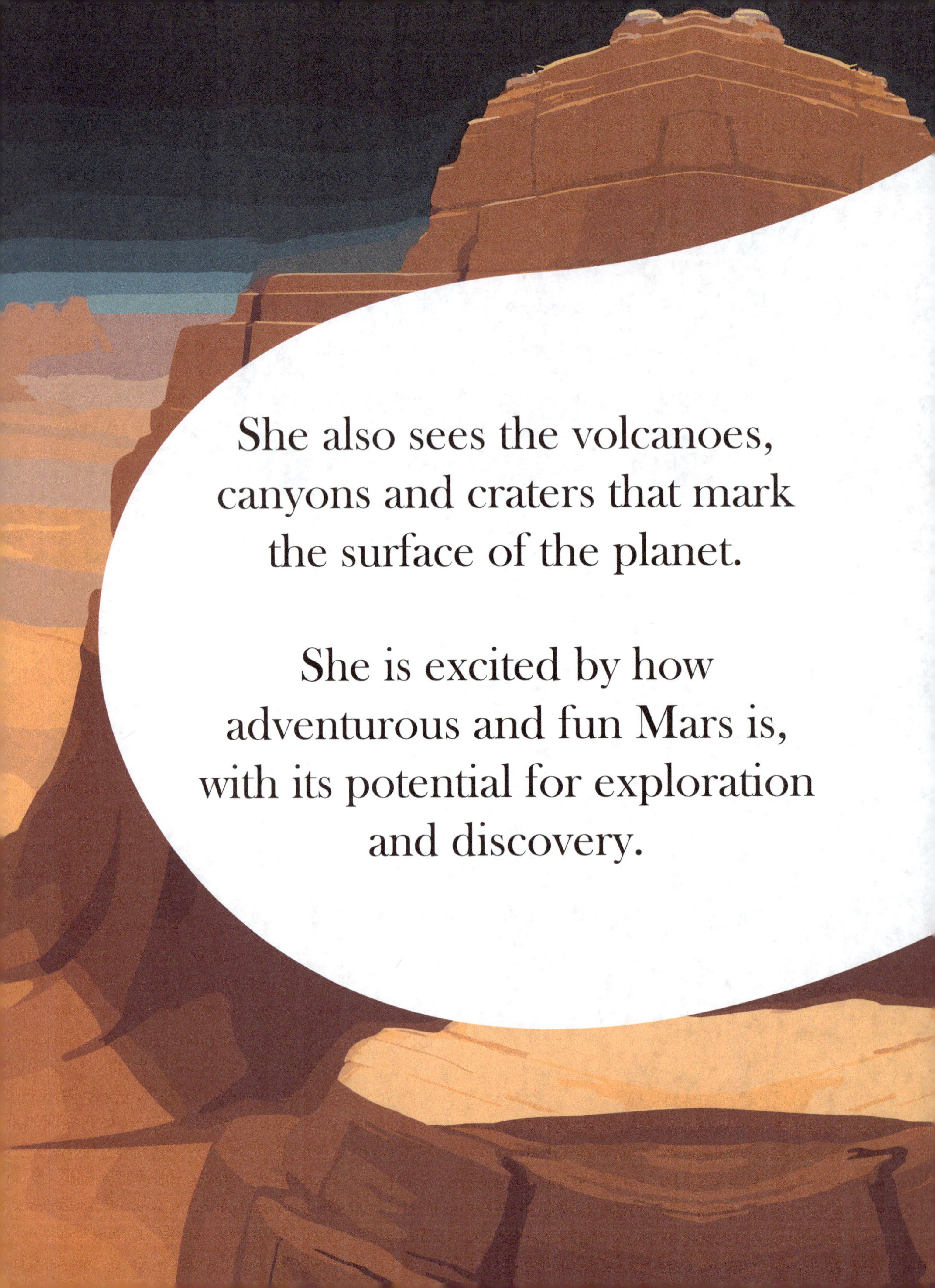
She also sees the volcanoes,
canyons and craters that mark
the surface of the planet.

She is excited by how
adventurous and fun Mars is,
with its potential for exploration
and discovery.

Luna learns that Mars is a very adventurous and fun planet that has many possibilities to explore.

She also learns that being brave and adventurous can help her overcome challenges and achieve her goals.

Luna falls asleep with a book
about Jupiter and dreams of
flying to the fifth planet from
the sun.

Hi! I'm Jupi

She meets a wise and friendly
alien named Jupi who shows
her around the planet.

She learns that Jupiter
is the largest and most
powerful planet in the solar
system, with a massive
atmosphere, a strong magnetic
field and dozens of moons.

She also sees the Great Red Spot, a giant storm that has been raging for centuries.

She is impressed by how powerful Jupiter is, with its force and influence.

Luna learns that Jupiter is a
very powerful planet that has
many mysteries to solve.

She also learns that being wise
and friendly can help her learn
from others and make friends.